The Parent's Guide to Teen Mental Health

Table of Contents

Chapter 1. Introduction

Special Report: "The Parent's Guide to Teen Mental Health"

Navigating the tumultuous teen years can be a challenge for both parents and teenagers alike. Our Special Report, "The Parent's Guide to Teen Mental Health," is a benchmark resource that you simply cannot afford to bypass. It's your compass in the ever-complicated world of puberty, hormones, mood swings, and the all-important issue of teen mental health! Far from being a humdrum or overwhelmingly technical read, our guide promises to be a beacon of light, offering easy to understand advice, practical strategies, and heartwarming stories of triumph and perseverance. This is not just another document, but a lifeline reaching out to help you build a strong, healthy relationship with your teen. Just by turning the pages, you will not only unlock the keys to understanding your teen's mental health, but also help pave the path to their brighter, healthier future!

Chapter 2. Understanding the Teenage Brain

The teenage years represent an intriguing period of drastic physical, emotional, and cognitive transformations. These changes not only frame their personalities, but also play a significant role in how they interact with the world around them. To decode this complex web, we must first look under the hood at the workings of the teenage brain.

2.1. The Neurological Transformation

From birth through the early years of life, our brain develops at an astonishing rate, laying down neural pathways and strengthening connections. By the time we reach adolescence, it undergoes another developmental leap, pruning away unused connections and bolstering others. This process, known as 'synaptic pruning,' allows the teenage brain to become more efficient and concentrated. In this stage, it's not about producing new neurons, but rather about fine-tuning and streamlining the connections.

2.2. The Role of the Prefrontal Cortex

A key player in this developmental period is the prefrontal cortex. Responsible for logical thinking, judgment, and impulse control, this part of the brain doesn't fully mature until the mid to late twenties. This gradual maturation process is why teenagers, despite their physical growth, still have the propensity to make decisions based on emotion rather than rational thought.

During adolescence, the prefrontal cortex is similarly undergoing synaptic pruning, fine-tuning its circuits. However, the painstaking pace at which it matures often results in impulsivity and poor decision making, leading teens to engage in risky behaviors. It's important to remember that this doesn't indicate irresponsibility or defiance, but rather a brain structure still learning to find its balance.

2.3. Hormonal Impact

It's impossible to discuss the teenage brain without delving into the highs and lows of hormonal changes. Two key hormones at play during adolescence are testosterone and estrogen. Both these hormones contribute to drastic physical changes like the deepening of the voice, onset of menstruation, and growth of bodily hair. While this is happening, these hormones also play a significant role in the emotional and behavioral changes observed during this transitional period.

Cortisol, the stress hormone, also tends to surge during this period. This can contribute to feelings of anxiety, stress and can exacerbate mood swings, making the teen years an emotionally turbulent time.

2.4. The Sleep-Wake Cycle Shift

Many parents complain about their teens staying up late into the night and struggling to wake up early for school. It's not defiance – it's due to a shift in the circadian rhythm during adolescence. Melatonin, the hormone responsible for inducing sleep, releases roughly two hours later in teenagers than in children or adults. This shift leads to teenagers being naturally inclined to stay up and wake up later. The mismatch between their biological clocks and school schedules can lead to sleep deprivation, further intensifying mood swings and cognitive challenges.

2.5. The Allure of Risk-taking

The amalgamation of an underdeveloped prefrontal cortex, a surge in hormones, and a heightened response to reward makes teenagers more prone to risk-taking behaviors. While this can be a cause for concern, it's important to remember that risk-taking isn't necessarily a negative trait. It can lead to new experiences, learning opportunities, and growth. However, it becomes problematic when it results in harmful consequences, such as alcohol consumption, drug use, reckless driving, or unsafe sexual practices.

The key is open dialogue and reinforcement of safer choices that allows teenagers to feed their natural curiosity without endangering themselves or others around them.

2.6. The Importance of Nurturing

Despite the rearrangements and reorganizations within the teenage brain, it's still remarkably flexible. This flexibility, or 'neuroplasticity,' means that the adolescent brain can be influenced – both positively and negatively.

Positive experiences such as supportive parenting, healthy relationships, and meaningful connections can help to wire the developing adolescent brain healthily. On the other hand, negative situations like traumatic events, substance abuse, or neglect can have a deleterious effect on the brain's development.

2.7. Building Bridges: Communication & Understanding

During this crucial period of development, understanding the teenage brain can facilitate more compassionate parent-teen relationships. Acceptance, empathy, and open lines of communication can encourage mutual respect and contribute to a more harmonious family dynamic.

Understanding the changes occurring in the teenage brain doesn't mean excusing negative behavior. Instead, it equips you with the insight to handle these instances more constructively.

Embrace the changes, the challenges and even the conflicts that come along with the offspring's transition from childhood to adulthood. After all, it is a passage to human development and a training ground for future life skills. The more informed you are about the way the all-important teenage brain works, the better you'll be able to foster an environment that supports your teenager on their journey to becoming a happy, healthy adult.

Chapter 3. The Impact of Social Media on Teen Mental Health

In an era where social media is an integral part of our daily lives, it's crucial to understand its effects on teenage mental health. With platforms like Facebook, Instagram, Snapchat, and TikTok forging dynamic, and at times overwhelming, spaces for interaction, we are compelled to examine their impacts, both positive and negative, on teens.

3.1. A Contemporary Landscape

In our technologically centered society, social media is more than just a means of communication; it's a cultural staple. It establishes trends and norms, determines the course of political, economic, and social discourse, and provides a platform for connection and expression for people all over the world, particularly teens. On one hand, it can facilitate camaraderie and creativity, but on the other, it can be a breeding ground for peer pressure, comparison, and cyberbullying, all of which impact a teen's mental health.

3.2. The Good: Connection, Community and Self-Expression

One of the major advantages of social media comes from its power to create networks of support and community-building. It exposes teens to a diverse range of perspectives, experiences, and cultures, contributing to a more holistic understanding of the world. Through shared interests, they can connect with groups, pages, and individuals, which can provide emotional support and consolation. It also offers them platforms to express themselves creatively and intellectually, therefore fostering self-confidence.

3.3. The Bad: Cyberbullying and Peer Pressure

Unfortunately, social media also harbors pitfalls that can adversely affect teen mental health. Cyberbullying is a significant issue, with individuals feeling more emboldened to engage in hurtful behavior behind the anonymity of a screen. It can severely impact self-esteem and lead to depression, anxiety, and in extreme cases, suicidal thoughts. Similarly, peer pressure can occur in subtle ways online, encouraging risky behaviors such as substance abuse or reckless actions to gain social acceptance.

3.4. The Ugly: Comparison and Social Media Anxiety

Comparison is an unavoidable part of using social media. Teens often perceive the lives presented on platforms like Instagram or Facebook as authentic, despite their often curated nature. This can lead to feelings of inadequacy, self-doubt, and low self-esteem. Moreover, the constant availability and expectation to be perennially 'online' can lead to social media anxiety, a form of stress related to maintaining a particular image, responding immediately to messages, or feelings of missing out.

3.5. Impact on Body Image

The portrayal of unrealistic 'ideal' body standards on social media can significantly impact teens' body image and self-perception. Feelings of dissatisfaction and negative self-comparison can occur, leading to self-esteem issues and potentially contributing to eating disorders. It's crucial that teens understand the heavily filtered and edited reality presented online.

3.6. The Role of Parents

To help mitigate these potential hazards, parents need to engage with their teens on social media usage. Open dialogue about online experiences can help teens overcome challenges and develop healthy digital habits. Parents can lay out expectations, privacy measures, and time limits for social media use, and regularly check-in to understand their teen's online interactions.

3.7. Conclusion

While no definitive stance categorizes social media as wholly good or bad, its power is undeniable, particularly over the sometimes vulnerable population of teenagers. It's pivotal for parents, educators, and policy-makers to understand and navigate these impacts on teen mental health. A balance between fostering online creativity and connection, and warding off potential harm, is intricately tied to the wellbeing of the next digital natives generation.

Chapter 4. Signs and Symptoms: When to Seek Help

Understanding your teenager might sometimes feel akin to cracking the enigma code. Subtle changes in behavior and mood swings are a natural part of adolescent behavior, and discerning when these shifts cross the boundary into concerning territory can be a daunting task. This comprehensive guide is designed to help you identify signs and symptoms that might indicate the need for professional help and intervention.

4.1. Identifying Changes in Behavior

Primarily, it's necessary to recognize that occasional moodiness and irritability can be normal for teenagers. However, when these changes become the norm rather than the exception, there might be cause for concern. Changes in behavior that can point towards a possible mental health condition include a pronounced shift in their sleeping patterns, an abrupt loss of interest in activities they once enjoyed, substantial weight loss or gain, and a deteriorating academic performance.

Furthermore, watch out for unusual agitation, restlessness, or anger. If your teenager starts expressing feelings of worthlessness, guilt, or becomes overly critical of themselves, it may be a signal of a deeper issue. Other worrying signs include: unexplained aches and pains, a decline in energy or motivation, difficulty concentrating, feelings of unhappiness or despair, and an increased sensitivity to rejection or failure. If your teenager displays a significant number of these symptoms and these persist for more than two weeks, it is sensible to seek professional advice.

4.2. Analyzing Mood Shifts

Teenagers are invariably subject to hormonal changes that can result in significant mood swings. However, mood changes can also indicate a mental health issue when they are extreme or uncharacteristic of your teen's usual behavior. You may observe your teen experiencing periods of great excitement, during which they have boundless energy, followed by episodes of depression or apathy. These kinds of 'highs' and 'lows' could suggest a mood disorder, such as bipolar disorder.

Indicators of possible depression include persistent feelings of sadness, frustration, or anger. Your teenager may cry frequently, have trouble sleeping, or sleep excessively. Depression might also present as unexplained physical complaints, such as a constant stomachache or headache. If your teen displays these symptoms for an extended period, it would be prudent to seek professional assistance.

4.3. Noticing Social Changes

A shift in your teenager's social interactions can also signal potential mental health issues. If they suddenly start avoiding social activities they usually enjoy, consistently isolate themselves from their friends and family, or display a noticeable lack of interest in cultivating relationships, it may point towards social anxiety, depression, or other disorders.

You might also observe significant changes in their school performance. A sudden drop in grades, dwindling interest in extracurricular activities, frequent absences, or troubles with the school law and order can be significant indicators of a deeper issue at hand.

4.4. Spotting Risky Behavior

Perhaps most alarmingly, a sudden engagement in risk-taking behavior may also signal mental distress. This could present as reckless driving, unsafe sex, substance abuse, or other dangerous activities. Conversely, uncharacteristic concerns about safety and avoidance of routine activities could indicate an anxiety disorder.

4.5. Expressions of Distress

Expressions of distress, such as self-harm, threats or discussions about suicide, and writing or drawing about death, are serious indicators of mental health issues requiring immediate professional attention.

Ultimately, it's crucial to approach these situations with empathy, understanding, and patience, while recognizing that mental health conditions are treatable. If you have identified any potentially concerning behaviors, it is crucial to seek a professional evaluation. The road to recovery may be challenging, but with your support, your teen can navigate it successfully. Remember, every teenager's journey is unique, and what works for one may not necessarily work for all. As such, tailored advice from a professional is paramount in addressing teen mental health.

Chapter 5. Building open Communication: The Art of Listening

Many of the issues that surround teen mental health stem from a lack of open communication or a misunderstanding of how such communication should function. Being a parent, more than just a source of authority and provision, you should also be an active participant in your youth's world.

Building open communication starts with understanding and mastering the art of listening. Listening is a critical cornerstone of effective communication, but it's far more than simply hearing the words spoken. Involving emotional and mental processes, it demands patience, focus, empathy, and much more.

5.1. Understanding Active Listening

Active listening involves focusing entirely on the speaker, absorbing both the content of their words and the context in which they speak them. It requires an understanding of their perspective and feelings on the issue being discussed. It's about respect—showing by your actions that you value what they're saying. Active listening, essentially, means absorbing, understanding, and responding to the total message being sent.

To practice active listening, firstly, eliminate any distractions. Shut off the phone, turn off television—even move to a quieter place if necessary. Display receptive body language: maintain eye contact, nod in understanding, and lean in slightly closer to show that you're fully engaged. Moreover, paraphrase or restate what your teen says in your own words. This encourages clarification, demonstrating to your teen that you're interested in fully grasping their thoughts.

5.2. Avoiding Judgment and Criticism

It's critical to create a safe space where your teen can express thoughts and emotions without fear of judgment or criticism. Remember that their experiences, though different from yours, are equally real and significant. Instead of immediately sharing your thoughts, take a moment to digest what your teen has shared with you. This allows for consideration of their feelings and fosters mutual respect.

Validating their feelings doesn't mean agreeing with their views or decisions; it means acknowledging their experiences as important aspects of their identity. To disagree without invalidating, ensure to address the issue at hand, not the person. That way, you constructively criticize wrong actions, while still appreciating your child's unique identity.

5.3. Nurturing Emotional Honesty

Teens often grapple with a myriad of complex emotions, which they may find difficult to articulate. To nurture emotional honesty, encourage your teen to express emotions freely. It might be helpful to teach them that it's perfectly okay to be confused about one's feelings sometimes—after all, emotions are complicated.

Try to model emotional honesty for them and explain how you process your feelings as well. When giving responses, ensure your own emotional honesty shines through. This not only promotes effective communication but aids in the development of your teen's emotional intelligence.

5.4. Asking Open-Ended Questions

Active listening involves asking open-ended questions. Unlike closed-ended questions, these allow the speaker to express their thoughts more fully and delve deeper into the matter at hand. They encourage a fuller engagement in the conversation, and pave the way for greater understanding. Examples of open-ended questions include, "How did that make you feel?" or "What was your interpretation of the situation?"

5.5. Harnessing the Power of Silence

In communication, silence is as powerful as words. Sometimes, all your teen needs is for you to sit quietly in understanding, giving them room to process their thoughts and feelings. Silence shows that you're patient, that you have faith in their ability to handle their emotions. It gives them time to explore their thoughts further, and perhaps even discover solutions on their own.

It needs to be emphasized, though, that there's a difference between supportive silence and the silence driven by neglect or resentment. The former is attentive, engaged, and respectful; it serves as a cushion – soft, safe, and non-intrusive. The latter, on the other hand, breeds distance and discomfort.

In the end, cultivating open communication is not an overnight task—it's the result of consistent effort and understanding. You're not expected to be perfect, but with every effort, you move closer to building a stronger and healthier bond with your teen. Keep in mind that as much as this is about your teen, it's also about you as a parent. Mastering the art of listening will not just benefit your teen; it'll also aid in your personal growth. Remember, skillful listening is key to successful communication.

Remember, this is an ongoing journey, and while there will be inevitable bumps along the road, consistent and mindful effort from your end will help establish a strong, healthy connection between you and your adolescent.

Chapter 6. Addressing Self-Esteem and Body Image Issues

The teenage years are a time of significant change and development, both physically and mentally. This period is often synonymous with issues related to self-esteem and body image as teenagers try to navigate their changing selves in an appearance-conscious world.

6.1. Understanding Self-esteem and Body Image

Self-esteem refers to how individuals perceive their individual value or self-worth. It influences every aspect of life, from academic performance to relationships. On the other hand, body image is the mental picture people have of their body, combined with the feelings one has about their appearance, size, and shape.

It's important to note that body image isn't only about how one perceives their physical attributes; it also impacts their confidence, self-esteem, and overall mental health. It's a complex feature of self-identity and has a profound impact on a teenager's self-esteem.

6.2. Factors Influencing Self-esteem and Body Image

Numerous factors contribute to the formation of self-esteem and body image in teens, ranging from cultural influence to media exposure, peer pressure, and genetic predisposition.

Cultural ideals and norms dictate what is considered 'beautiful' or 'appealing,' and deviations from these norms can result in adverse self-evaluation and self-view. The media, through advertising and content, tend to promote unrealistic beauty and fitness standards, causing many teenagers to feel dissatisfied with their looks. Peer comparisons and negative feedback can also encourage poor self-esteem and a distorted view about one's body.

Genetic factors and familial patterns can play a critical role as well. Hormonal changes during puberty can cause rapid fluctuations in weight and physical appearance, affecting a teenager's body image.

6.3. Signs of Poor Self-Esteem and Negative Body Image

It's crucial to be proactive in detecting any signs of low self-esteem and negative body image in your teenager. Signs could vary from noticeable behavioral changes such as withdrawing from social activities, changes in eating habits, or displaying obsessive tendencies towards their appearance.

Note that changes in body dissatisfaction do not always lead to severe problems. Still, it is essential to intervene if negative body image is causing your teen considerable distress or leading to unhealthy behaviors.

6.4. How to Boost Self-esteem and Positive Body Image

As a parent, you hold a remarkable position to inspire positive self-esteem and body image in your teen. Here are some tips:

Encourage a Healthy Relationship with Food: Instill a balanced approach to nutrition. Teach your teen to look at food as a source of nourishment, not linking its consumption directly to weight gain or loss.

Promote Physical Activities: Exercise helps to improve body image. It boosts mood, helps in managing stress, and promotes a sense of achievement that can significantly enhance self-esteem.

Encourage Open Discussion: Create an open and non-judgmental atmosphere at home, where your teen feels comfortable talking about their feelings or apprehensions regarding body image or their appearance.

Boost their Confidence: Value their abilities and contributions, and guide them to recognize their potentials. Boost their confidence by focusing on their strengths instead of their weaknesses.

Maintain open communication: Teens most often may not directly express their feelings of inadequacy. You need to establish open communication, encouraging them to voice their concerns and reassuring them of your support.

Raise Media Awareness: Teach your teens to develop a critical perspective towards media images which often promote unrealistic and unattainable ideals of beauty. Help your teen understand that their self-worth is much more than just physical appearance.

6.5. Seeking Professional Help

While the above strategies are beneficial, there may still be moments when professional intervention is necessary. If your teen's body dissatisfaction is causing severe distress, leading to disruptive behaviors or thoughts of self-harm, it's crucial to seek help from a mental health professional.

Remember, the journey towards positive self-esteem and a healthy body image is a process. With patience, understanding, and proactive strategies, parents can guide their teens brilliantly through this challenging phase of life. Your role in shaping their self-identity cannot be overstated. Aim to be there for them, open and supportive, as they navigate their path towards adulthood.

Chapter 7. Coping Techniques: Tools for Stress and Anxiety

Managing stress and anxiety is a vital skill for teenagers. Teen years are filled with changes and challenges, from physical changes to new social and academic pressures, which can often lead to feelings of stress and anxiety. Having a toolbox of coping techniques can be an incredibly valuable asset for teenagers during these trying times. The following tools and techniques are designed to help your teen navigate and manage stress and anxiety effectively.

7.1. Understanding Stress and Anxiety

Before diving into the various techniques to manage stress and anxiety, it's important to understand what stress and anxiety are. Stress is typically a reaction to a specific trigger or set of circumstances, often dubbed a 'stressor'. This could be an upcoming test, a disagreement with a friend, or an over-packed schedule.

Anxiety, on the other hand, often happens without any discernible trigger or stressor. Whereas stress tends to subside when the stressor is removed, anxiety often lingers and can interfere with daily life.

Knowing the difference between the two can help your teen customize coping strategies that best suit their needs.

7.2. Recognizing Stress and Anxiety Signs

Helping your teen understand the signs of stress and anxiety is the first step towards managing it. Usual signs of stress include difficulty sleeping, headaches, changes in eating habits, mood swings, difficulty concentrating, etc. Physical symptoms of anxiety might overlap with those of stress but usually include feelings of restlessness and excessive worrying.

7.3. Keeping a Stress Diary

One practical tool for managing stress and anxiety is keeping a Stress Diary. Encourage your teen to note down what causes them stress, the feelings they experience, and their reactions. This diary will help identify the recurring situations that lead to stress, the body's response to it, and can assist in devising the best coping mechanisms.

7.4. Breathing Exercises

Deep breathing stimulates the body's relaxation response, leading to a decrease in heart rate and blood pressure, providing immediate stress relief.

A simple method to practice is the 4-7-8 technique. This involves breathing in for a count of 4, holding the breath for 7 seconds, and exhaling for 8 seconds. This cycle should be repeated until the individual experiences a calming effect.

7.5. Physical Activity

Physical activity releases endorphins that can help your teen feel happier and more relaxed. It also increases focus and improves mood, acting as a natural stress-reliever. Activities can range from taking a brisk walk, yoga, dancing, to more intensive forms like team sports or running.

7.6. Healthy Eating Habits

Diet has a critical role in regulating mood. Advocate for a balanced diet, rich in fruits, vegetables, lean proteins, and complex carbohydrates. Limiting caffeine and sugar intake can also help manage stress and anxiety, as these substances can contribute to feelings of jitteriness and unease.

7.7. Good Sleep Hygiene

Insufficient sleep can intensify feelings of stress and anxiety. Establishing good sleep hygiene principles, such as reducing screen time before bed, maintaining a consistent sleep routine, and ensuring a restful sleep environment, can significantly enhance the quality of rest.

7.8. Mindfulness and Meditation

Mindfulness involves focusing your mind on the present moment, which can help reduce feelings of stress and anxiety. Simple ways to practice mindfulness include mindful eating, mindful walking, or even spending time in nature. Techniques such as guided imagery or progressive muscle relaxation can also be beneficial.

7.9. Social Support

Encourage your teen to lean on their social support system – friends, family, or teachers who can provide emotional support during stressful times. Having someone to talk with about their concerns can ease anxiety-inducing thoughts.

7.10. Professional Help

If your teen's stress or anxiety levels are overwhelming to the point where they interfere with daily life, it may be time to seek professional support. A mental health professional can provide your teen with support and further tools to cope with their stress and anxiety.

Moving forward, it's important to remember that stress and anxiety are part of life, and even more so during the teenage years. However, equipping your teen with these tools and coping strategies can set the stage for a healthier, happier, and more resilient future.

Chapter 8. The Role of Nutrition and Exercise in Mental Health

The harrowing world of teenagehood can be further complicated when mental health concerns start to rear their heads. Your teen may be grappling with mood swings, anxiety, or depression, all of which take a toll on their wellbeing. Amidst this, one aspect not to be overlooked is their nutritional habits and physical activities, which play a pivotal role in shaping their mental health.

8.1. Understanding the Nutrition-Mental Health Connection

The food your teen consumes affects not only their physical health, but also their mental health. Building upon the "you are what you eat" adage, it is crucial for parents to understand the significance of their child's nutritional intake, as it directly impacts both their mood and cognitive functioning.

Research has found a direct correlation between diet quality and mental health. Specifically, a diet high in processed foods with excessive sugar and unhealthy fats unsurprisingly triggers a negative impact on mental health. Junks foods, while enticing taste-wise to many teenagers, may heighten the risk of depression, anxiety and other mental health disorders, due to their effects on blood sugar, inflammation, and brain function.

Conversely, a balanced diet filled with whole grains, proteins, fruits, and vegetables can work wonders for your teen's mental health. Nutrients like omega-3 fatty acids, antioxidants, B vitamins, and probiotics are especially beneficial, contributing to improved mood, decreased anxiety, and enhanced cognitive functioning.

8.2. The Importance of Exercise in Teen Mental Health

Just as a balanced diet is paramount for mental wellbeing, so too is regular physical activity. Exercise releases endorphins, popularly referred to as "feel-good hormones," which empirically helps in mood elevation and stress reduction.

There exists an established correlation between regular physical activity and lower rates of depression and anxiety across all age groups, teens included. Encouraging your teen to engage in some form of exercise, be it playing a sport, walking, running, or cycling for at least an hour a day can contribute significantly to their mental health.

Exercise also aids in sleep regulation, another crucial aspect of mental health. Teenagers who engage in regular physical activity are more likely to sleep well, which in turn positively impacts their mental health.

8.3. Incorporating Nutritional Changes

It can be challenging for parents to balance providing a nutritious diet with accommodating their teen's food preferences. Here are some strategies to help:

1. Start by making minor changes rather than dramatic shifts. Gradually reduce the servings of processed foods and replace them with healthier options.

2. Encourage your teen to be involved in meal planning and

preparation. This not only teaches them handy skills, but also gives them a sense of ownership and increases the chances of them eating healthy.

3. Make fruits and vegetables interesting. Use them in smoothies, salads, and dips to make them more enticing.

Remember, Rome wasn't built in a day. Similarly, changes in dietary habits don't happen overnight. It's key to stay persistent and patient.

8.4. Cultivating a Love for Physical Activity

Getting your teen to be physically active can be a bit tricky, especially in this digital age where screens often steal the spotlight. Here are some tips:

1. Find a sport or activity they love. If they enjoy what they're doing, they're more likely to stick with it.

2. Model active behavior. If your teen sees you being active, they're more likely to follow suit.

3. Create opportunities for family physical activity. This can range from taking family walks after dinner to going on hiking trips over the weekend.

4. Break up sedentary time. Encourage your teen to take short active breaks during long stretches of screen time.

8.5. Role of Routine and Structure

Implementing a framework of routine meals and exercise times can offer a sense of security and regularity to your teen's life. Structure is comforting and can help enhance their stability and focus, which ultimately supports mental health.

8.6. Navigating Pushback

Resistance is natural. Your teen might resist these changes, especially if they're used to a certain way of eating or living. It's important to approach this with empathy and conversation, acknowledging their feelings while demonstrating the benefits over their current lifestyle.

In conclusion, understanding the critical role of nutrition and exercise for your teenager's mental health is the first step to proactively supporting them. Balancing dietary needs with physical activity creates a robust defense against the dark clouds of depression, anxiety, and mood swings. With patience, persistence, and understanding, you can guide your teenager towards a healthier lifestyle that not only benefits their physical health, but also supports their developing mind.

Chapter 9. When School Becomes Overwhelming: Dealing with Academic Pressure

The youthful years of our lives are often the most impactful, molding our perceptions and shaping our future. However, it is also a time when significant pressures, specifically academic ones, can occur. These pressures can often lead to a deterioration in mental health if not appropriately recognized and addressed.

9.1. Identifying Academic Stress Signs

Recognizing the signs of academic stress is the first step to handling it. It's important to be observant, looking out for changes in behavior, academic performance, or sociability. The following indicators could likely suggest that your teen is experiencing academic pressure:

- Drastic changes in sleep patterns or issues with insomnia

- A significant decline in grades or increased difficulty with understanding content

- Increased irritability and tension

- Regular headaches, stomachaches, or other physical ailments

- Withdrawal from activities or friends they once enjoyed

- Frequent expressions of negativity or apprehension towards school.

These signs aren't exclusive or definitive proof that your teen is grappling with academic pressure, but they should be taken as signal flags urging for future evaluation.

9.2. Understanding the Sources

After identifying the signs, understanding the origins of academic stress is crucial. It may come from a variety of sources:

- High Expectations: The pressure to perform, fulfill certain standards or gain parental approval is a significant stress source.

- Workload: Overwhelming amounts of homework, projects, or constant testing can contribute to stress levels.

- Future Anxiety: Concerns about college admissions, career paths, and life after high school can add to the burden.

- School Environment: Bullying, peer pressure, or feeling isolated can cause further stress.

- Personal Issues: Problems outside the educational sphere, such as family issues or breakups, can amplify pressure.

It's essential to talk openly with your teen about these potential stressors and observe any changes to their academic or personal life that may be influencing their mental health.

9.3. Strong Communication and Rebuilding Confidence

In the face of academic pressure, forging a strong line of communication with your adolescent is fundamental. Here are a few strategies to do that:

- Regular Discussions: Make a habit of discussing their school day, assignments, and friends in a non-intrusive manner.

- Be Understanding: If your teen opens up about their stress, be empathetic, avoid judgment, and offer strength and support.

- Encourage Healthy Perceptions: Reinforce the notion that their worth is not determined by their grades and that it's okay to make mistakes.

- Offer Help: If they're struggling with their academics, assist them or consider professional tutoring.

Building confidence assists in combating academic pressures. Allow your child to voice their opinions, make decisions, and accept praise to improve their self-esteem.

9.4. Fostering a Balanced Life

Encourage your child to lead a balanced life, balancing study time with extracurricular activities, relaxation, and socialization. Below are strategies to foster this balance:

- Encourage Healthy Habits: Regular physical exercise, a wholesome diet, and appropriate sleep can help your teen deal with stress.

- Hobbies and Interests: Encourage hobbies and interests outside of academics. It provides a welcome diversion, enhances skills, and promotes well-being.

- Socialize: Encourage friendships and positive social interaction, which can play a pivotal role in stress relief.

9.5. Seeking Professional Assistance

Despite your best efforts, there may be situations where professional assistance is necessary. Look out for prolonged symptoms of stress or if your teen's mental health poses a concern. Consider consulting with a school counselor, psychologist, or other mental health professional. They can help evaluate the situation and suggest individualized steps that can be critical to your teen's well-being.

In summary, dealing with academic pressures involves identifying stress signs, understanding the sources, building strong communication, fostering a balanced life, and seeking professional help when necessary. Above all, it is crucial to remind your teen that they are loved, valued, and capable of more than they would ever know, irrespective of their academic performance. In doing so, you can help pave the way for a resilient and successful future.

Chapter 10. Helping Your Teen Build Resilience

Resilience: The capacity to recover quickly from difficulties, to bounce back from adversity. It's a quality we would all love to instill in our teens. However, the question is—how? This section offers detailed strategies and tools to help your teen develop resilience, taking them, and you, on a journey that will leave them better equipped to face life's challenges head-on.

10.1. Understanding Resilience

Before we dive into how you can help your teen build resilience, it's important to understand what resilience really means. Contrary to some beliefs, resilience is not about avoiding difficulties or suppressing feelings. Instead, it's about learning to adapt to life's misfortunes and stresses. Resilience is the ability to pick yourself up after a fall, dust yourself off, and move forward with renewed vigor.

Teens with resilience are able to effectively navigate through life and handle stressors. They show determination and strength when faced with adversity. Building resilience does not mean that teens will not experience difficulty or distress, but it does equip them with the skills to manage those difficulties when they arise.

10.2. The Role of Resilience in Teen Mental Health

Resilience plays a significant role in teen mental health. The adolescent years are a time of many changes – physical, emotional, and social. These changes can sometimes be overwhelming. Resilience helps teens manage these changes and the associated stress.

Teens who are resilient have healthier ways to cope with stress, such as using problem-solving skills and seeking out support when needed. This can help protect them from various mental health issues including anxiety and depression. Building resilience is an essential aspect of promoting good mental health in teenagers.

10.3. Building Blocks of Resilience

Now that we have a clear understanding of what resilience is and what it implies for teens, let's delve into the building blocks that help in the creation of resilience.

1. Emotion Regulation: Training teens to understand and manage their emotions can help build resilience. This might involve teaching them to identify different emotions, understand how emotions influence their behavior, and implement coping strategies when they're feeling overwhelmed.

2. Positive Relationships: Strong, positive, and supportive relationships, both within the family and outside, can greatly contribute to resilience.

3. Problem-Solving Skills: Teaching teens to make informed decisions, solve problems effectively, and think critically can boost their resilience.

4. Self-Esteem and Confidence: It's critical for teens to have a positive image of themselves. Parents can promote this by affirming their strengths, encouraging their efforts, and helping them recognize and celebrate their achievements.

==⇒ Practical Strategies to Develop Resilience in Teens

Here are some practical strategies you can use to help your teen develop resilience:

1. Model Resilience: Possibly the most effective strategy is to model resilience yourself. Show your teen how you effectively handle stress and solve problems, allowing them to see you bounce back from setbacks.

2. Foster a Positive Home Environment: Create a positive and loving home environment that encourages open communication and problem-solving.

3. Encourage Healthy Risk-Taking: Encourage your teen to try new things, and help them understand that failure is just an opportunity to learn.

4. Teach Coping Skills: Equip your teen with various coping mechanisms, such as breathing exercises for stress, prioritizing tasks for overwhelming days, and good sleep hygiene for better rest and stress management.

5. Encourage an Active Lifestyle: An active lifestyle has been proven to reduce stress and improve mental health. Encouraging your teen to engage in physical activities they enjoy can significantly boost their resilience.

10.4. Conclusion: Resilience - A Journey, not a Destination

Resilience is a journey, not a one-off event. It takes time to cultivate resilience, just as it takes time for a tree to take root and grow. Equipping your teen with a strong foundation of resilience skills will not only help them navigate their teen years but also set them up for success in adulthood. Show patience, exhibit understanding, and provide consistent support — and remember, you are not alone in this journey!

As we wrap up this section, remember that fostering resilience is a collaborative process. It includes your teen, family, school, and even your wider community. So be patient and persistent, and soon you will see your teen emerge stronger, healthier and ready to face whatever life throws at them with resilience.

Chapter 11. Finding the Right Support: Therapies, Counselors, and Support Groups

Understanding the types of therapy, approaching counselors wisely, and harnessing the supportive power of peer groups can have a profound impact on a teen's mental well-being. Therefore, it is crucial to have comprehensive knowledge about these areas to better support your teen.

11.1. Types of Therapies

Understanding different forms of therapy can empower you to make informed decisions for your child. These vary in approach and focus, targeting specific issues your teen may be struggling with.

1. **Cognitive Behavioral Therapy (CBT)**: This widely prevalent form of therapy helps patients understand the interplay of thoughts, feelings, and behavior. It equips them with coping mechanisms to change thought patterns causing distress.

2. **Dialectical Behavior Therapy (DBT)**: DBT combines cognitive behavioral techniques with mindfulness. It is ideal for individuals who have difficulty controlling emotions and is often used for those struggling with self-harm and borderline personality disorder.

3. **Family Therapy**: It views issues in the context of family relationships and dynamics. It is beneficial when familial conditions contribute to the teen's mental health issue.

4. **Play Therapy**: Used primarily with younger children, it leverages

play as a medium for children to express emotions they might otherwise struggle with.

5. **Art Therapy**: Uses creative practices like drawing, painting, and sculpting to help express and understand emotions.

6. **Mindfulness-Based Therapies**: These leverage mindfulness practices as tools for managing thoughts and feelings effectively.

11.2. Finding and Working With the Right Therapist

Finding an appropriate therapist for your teen is crucial. Some key points to consider:

1. **Licensing and Credentials**: These can include Psychologist (PhD or PsyD), Licensed Clinical Social Worker (LCSW), Licensed Professional Counselor (LPC), or Psychiatrist (MD).

2. **Specialty**: Therapists have areas they specialize in, for example, teen anxiety or depression. Matching a therapist's expertise with the needs of your child is important.

3. **Approach and Philosophy**: Understanding a therapist's way of work, treatment methods, and philosophical orientation can provide insight into whether they are a good fit for your teen.

When you conduct an initial consultation, remember to ask about the therapist's approach, his/her comfort handling your teenager's specific issue, availability, and fees. Ask about the therapist's comfort discussing progress and feedback, success rate with similar situations, and their expectations from parents. Post-appointment, consider if your teen felt comfortable opening up to the therapist.

Remember, a good theraputic relationship can significantly impact the effectiveness of therapy.

11.3. Introduction to Support Groups

Support groups are a wonderful resource for adolescents grappling with mental health issues. They provide solace, understanding, and shared experiences. There are a wide variety of support groups available: for specific mental illnesses, general wellness, or secondary issues like living with a disability.

Choose a support group wisely. Ensure it's led by a licensed professional and that confidentiality is respected. Poorly run groups can do more harm than good.

While online support groups are a convenient alternative, face-to-face time can greatly contribute to the therapeutic process. Advantages of this include: the opportunity to learn from others' experiences, increased empathy, developing practical skills, lessened stigma, emotional catharsis, and increased self-esteem.

Ensure that any support group your teen joins is a safe, supportive environment. They should feel comfortable sharing and attaining the help they need.

Remember, as parents, you too may benefit from support groups specific to parents of teenagers with mental health issues. They offer advice and companionship from others in the same situation, reducing your sense of isolation.

In conclusion, providing the right support for your teen is of utmost importance. Understanding different therapy types, selecting a fitting therapist, and recognizing the value of support groups will not only improve the mental wellbeing of your teen but also strengthen your parent-child relationship. It's about paving a way for a brighter, healthier future.

www.ingramcontent.com/pod-product-compliance
Lightning Source LLC
Chambersburg PA
CBHW060853260726

48661CB00008B/3247